# NO KIDDING!

D0921845

# AROUND THE WORLD
## in Jokes, Riddles, and Games

**Marguerite Rodger**

Crabtree Publishing Company
www.crabtreebooks.com

# Crabtree Publishing Company
## www.crabtreebooks.com

**Author:** Marguerite Rodger

**Editorial Director:** Ellen Rodger

**Art Director:** Rosie Gowsell Pattison

**Editor:** Petrice Custance

**Proofreader:** Janine Deschenes

**Prepress technician:** Margaret Amy Salter

**Print and production coordinator:** Katherine Berti

Production coordinated by Plan B Book Packagers

**Photographs:**
Cover and title page: Kues/Shutterstock; p.2: Decorwith.me/ Shutterstock; p.4: Andrey Kuzmin/Shutterstock; p.5: Chaika/ Shutterstock; p.7 (UP): My Pokcik/Shutterstock; p.7 (LO): Oceloti/ Shutterstock; p.8: Digna/Shutterstock; p.9: Dzm1try/Shutterstock; p.10: Amero/Shutterstoc; p.11: Carolina K. Smith MD/Shutterstock; p.13: (LOLE): Memo Angeles/Shutterstock; p.13 (LOMID): Fixer00/ Shutterstock; p.14 (UP): Valzan/Shutterstock; p.14 (LO): Tamaretto/ Shutterstock; p.15 (MID): Scratch Video/Shutterstock; p.15(LO): Placid Gorilla/Shutterstock; p.16: JCJG Photography/Shutterstock; p.17 (MID): Maxicam/Shutterstock; p.17 (LO): Krol/Shutterstock; p.18 (UP): Koss 13/Shutterstock; p.18 (MID): Nixart/Shutterstock; p.19 (UP): Annette Shaff/Shutterstock; p.19 (LOLE): Svetlana Foote/ Shutterstock; p.19 (LORT): Georgiy Myakishev/Shutterstock; p.21 (MID): Terrace Studio/Shutterstock; p.21 (LO): Lonely/Shutterstock; p.22 (MID): CWB/Shutterstock; p.22 (LO): Marish/Shutterstock; p.23 (UP): Verzzh/Shutterstock; p.23 (LO): Julianna Million/Shutterstock; p.24: Tomacco/Shutterstock; p.25: Tomacco/Shutterstock; p.26 (MID): Sergei Primakov/Shutterstock; p.26 (LO): Tomacco/Shutterstock; p.28: Vectomart/Shutterstock; p.29: Real Illusion/Shutterstock; p.30: Viki2win/Shutterstock; p.31 (LOLE): Meunierd/Shutterstock; p.31 (LORT): 256786738/Shutterstock

## Library and Archives Canada Cataloguing in Publication

Rodger, Marguerite, author
        Around the world in jokes, riddles, and games / Marguerite Rodger.

(No kidding!)
Includes index.
Issued in print and electronic formats.
ISBN 978-0-7787-2388-2 (bound).--
ISBN 978-0-7787-2392-9 (paperback).--
ISBN 978-1-4271-1745-8 (html)

        1. Wit and humor. 2. Wit and humor, Juvenile. 3. Riddles, Juvenile. I. Title.

PN6151.R59 2016          jC818'.602          C2015-907476-2
                                             C2015-907477-0

## Library of Congress Cataloging-in-Publication Data

Names: Rodger, Marguerite, author.
Title: Around the world in jokes, riddles, and games / Marguerite Rodger.
Description: New York : Crabtree Publishing, 2016. | Series: No kidding! | Includes index.
Identifiers: LCCN 2016002786 (print) | LCCN 2016005298 (ebook) | ISBN 9780778723882 (reinforced library binding : alk. paper) | ISBN 9780778723929 (pbk. : alk. paper) | ISBN 9781427117458 (electronic HTML)
Subjects: LCSH: Wit and humor, Juvenile.
Classification: LCC PN6371.5 .R573 2016 (print) | LCC PN6371.5 (ebook) | DDC 818/.602--dc23
LC record available at http://lccn.loc.gov/2016002786

## Crabtree Publishing Company
www.crabtreebooks.com    1-800-387-7650

Printed in Canada/032016/EF20160210

**Published in Canada**
**Crabtree Publishing**
616 Welland Ave.
St. Catharines, Ontario
L2M 5V6

**Published in the United States**
**Crabtree Publishing**
PMB 59051
350 Fifth Avenue, 59th Floor
New York, New York 10118

**Published in the United Kingdom**
**Crabtree Publishing**
Maritime House
Basin Road North, Hove
BN41 1WR

**Published in Australia**
**Crabtree Publishing**
3 Charles Street
Coburg North
VIC, 3058

# CONTENTS

# CHAPTER 1
# FROM TOLEDO TO TIMBUKTU

**Have you ever noticed that laughter looks and sounds similar all around the world?** No matter where we're from, we all get a kick out of people and situations that are funny! Whether you're in Toledo or Timbuktu, laughter is pretty recognizable. Regardless of what language we speak, we can tell when another person is happy and laughing. Many researchers who study laughter say that it sounds and looks the way it does for an important reason: laughter helps us feel connected to one another. It turns out, laughter is one thing that bonds us together!

Earth is a big place. Our planet is home to many different **cultures** and traditions. There are thousands of different languages, but there is one that we are all familiar with: laughter. The language of laughter is **universal**, because we all know that laughter translates to happiness. From gut-busting giggles to shy, quiet smirks, laughing at a joke is something we can all relate to.

**Q** Where do pencils go on vacation?

**A** Pencilvania!

# CULTURALLY SENSITIVE

While laughing can bring us together, sometimes understanding a joke from another culture can be tricky! This is because jokes often evolve from language, geography, and history. For example, this joke may be easy for English-language speakers to figure out:

> **What is the longest word in the English language?**

> **Smiles—because there's a mile between its first and last letters!**

If English isn't your first language, or if you don't speak English at all, it might be difficult to understand why that joke is funny.

Sometimes, jokes are written or told with the purpose of laughing at other people, instead of with them. This can be really hurtful. We need to be especially careful when writing or telling jokes that are directed at other cultures, as these jokes can often reflect **stereotypes** instead of reality.

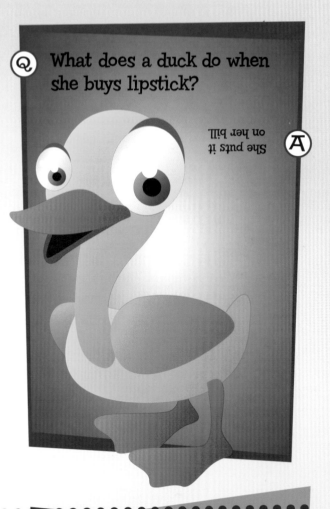

**Q** What does a duck do when she buys lipstick?

**A** She puts it on her bill.

## FUNNY BONE:

A smile doesn't always mean someone is happy or something is funny. In some Asian cultures, a smile can mean a person is sad, embarrassed, or uncomfortable. In North America, a smile is seen as a sign of happiness, but people will often smile in photos even if they aren't happy. Research shows that men also smile less than women.

# JOKE PARTS AND LABOR

In every language, jokes can be broken down into two main parts: the setup and the punch line.

**The Setup:** The setup of a joke is a sentence or two that gives the audience all the information necessary to be able to understand the joke. It can also be called the "foundation," because comedians use the setup to build up to the joke--similar to how buildings are built up from a foundation. In a traditional knock-knock joke, for example, the setup is that someone is knocking at the door.

**The Punch Line:** The punch line is the best part of the joke, because it is the part that contains the joke itself, and (hopefully) makes the audience laugh! It can also be called the laugh line. In a knock-knock joke, the punch line is always the last line of the joke, and the joke is usually made with the sound of the words.

Here's an example of an English knock-knock joke:

And here is a knock-knock joke in Spanish:

Knock, knock

Who's there?

Isabelle

Isabelle who?

Is a bell necessary on a bicycle?

Toc, toc (Knock, knock)

¿Quién es? (Who's there?)

Lola

¿Qué Lola? (Lola who?)

Los ladrones. (The thieves)

This joke is funny because the Spanish expression for "thieves" sounds a lot like the name Lola!

**Q** Why do the French eat snails?

**A** Because they don't like fast food.

**Q** What did the Pacific Ocean say to the Atlantic Ocean?

**A** Nothing, they just waved.

**Q** How does the tide come in to small beaches?

**A** In microwaves!

## FUNNY BONE:

Slapstick is a style of comedy often used in movies. It's a type of physical comedy. Actors use slapstick to make the audience laugh by purposely falling down stairs, colliding with each other, and throwing pies in one another's faces. Some of the best examples of slapstick comedians are the Three Stooges (American comedians), Jim Carrey (Canadian comedian), and Charlie Chaplin (British comedian). Slapstick was especially important during Charlie Chaplin's **heyday** in the 1920s, when movies were silent, and the actors had to make the audience laugh without using words!

# CHAPTER 2
# TRANSLATING LAUGHTER

**What has four eyes but cannot see?** Mississippi!! This joke is an example of a **riddle**. A riddle is a short sentence or poem with a hidden meaning. Riddles describe something without actually naming it, so the audience is left to guess the answer (which is often a funny punch line). Riddles can be fun to read and write, and can challenge your creative thinking. Here is an example of a simple riddle:

I stay in the corner, but travel around the world. What am I?

A stamp!

## RIDDLES OF THE WORLD

Riddles are popular all over the world. Writing and solving riddles gives you a chance to be clever with language. The answer is rarely the first word that comes to mind. In some parts of the world, such as Japan, riddles are used to challenge and stretch the imagination. In other places, such as the Asian island of Borneo, riddles teach important cultural lessons, rules, and morals. Sometimes, they are simply written to make an audience think, and then laugh with glee when they realize the answer!

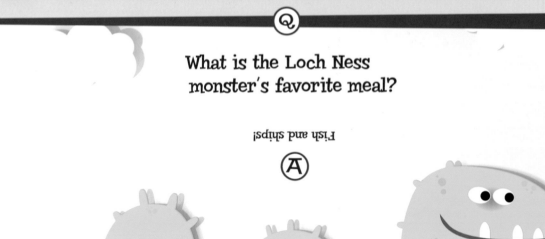

**Q** What is the Loch Ness monster's favorite meal?

**A** Fish and ships!

## WRITE YOUR OWN RIDDLE

Want to write your own riddle? Start with your answer. Write down some words that describe your answer. Then, use your notes to write a question that could have several answers. Remember, only one answer is both clever and correct. Your question can use **figurative language**, or figures of speech, to give the audience clues. Read on to learn more about using similes and metaphors in jokes!

## FUNNY BONE:

Droll is a word used to describe something that is funny in an unusual or silly way. The word comes from the French word for funny: drôle. It can also be used to describe a person who is acting like a joker or entertainer. The next time someone makes a joke that's so silly you'd like to roll your eyes, simply smile and say "Oh! How droll!"

## SIMILES ARE LIKE...

Using figurative language is a great way to get a crowd to laugh. Describing people or things in silly ways can create a great mental picture for your audience. Similes are a type of figurative language that allow you to compare two things using the words "like" or "as." Similes are often used in humor because they produce a strong, and often funny, visual image.

## SIMILE WHAT I MEAN?

Similes can be used to describe something in a pleasant way, such as, "Her voice was like the soft chirp of a dove." They can also be used in an **insulting** way, especially for humor. Take the French expression *elle chante comme un cheval de cirque*, which means, *she sings like a circus horse*. It's not the most flattering comparison, but this is what makes similes easy pickings for comedians.

## FUNNY BONE:

A photographer may use the expression "Say cheese!" to get the subjects of their photograph to crack a smile. Traditionally, the word "cheese" was used because saying the word caused people to open their mouths and show off some teeth (twisting their mouths into what—sort of—looked like a smile or a laugh). In other languages, "cheese" doesn't always translate. So what do photographers around the world use? In Bulgaria: "Zele," meaning "cabbage"; in Croatia: *ptičica*, meaning "little bird"; In Iran: بیس (saib), meaning "apple."

**Q** Why is the calendar so popular?

**A** It has a lot of dates.

**Q** Why do authors always feel cold?

**A** Because they are surrounded by drafts.

# LOST IN TRANSLATION?

Similes are used in many languages all over the world. Some similes are considered common expressions in one language, but may not translate well to others. For example, take the common English expression "you eat like a pig!" In some parts of the world, and in some cultures, pigs are considered special. Saying this expression to them would be very rude. Take a look at some other English similes and how they compare to similes from other cultures around the world:

| English Simile | Meaning | Similes from Around the World | Literal Translation |
|---|---|---|---|
| Shaking like a leaf! | To be scared or nervous. | Spanish: *Estar como un flan* | To be like pudding. |
| Fit as a fiddle! | To be very healthy. | Italian: *Sano come un pesce* | Healthy as a fish. |
| They're like two peas in a pod. | To be inseparable. | Russian: Они, как две капли воды | They are like two drops of water. |

Q Why did the police arrest the belt?

A Because it held up some pants.

# CHAPTER 3
# YOU ARE SO PUNNY!

**From knock-knock jokes to funny riddles, humor comes in many forms and flavors.** There's a type of humor and a form of joke that suits everyone. One thing that is common in almost all jokes (except for non-verbal, or silent comedy) is a good grasp of language.

## HOW PUNNY IS THAT?

A **pun** is a funny joke that uses words, called homonyms, that sound the same but have different meanings. This means that the word used as the punch line of the joke has more than one meaning, and can be interpreted in a funny way. Puns work in many different languages. They are often considered the simplest kind of joke. While they are pretty silly and can sometimes cause you to groan, your brain has to work extra hard to understand a pun. Puns can be complex and have several layers of meaning, and the audience has to understand the **wordplay** in the joke. Puns can be a great way to learn a new language. If you know one meaning of a word or expression, a pun can introduce a totally new way of looking at it!

Here's an example of a pun in Spanish:

¿Cuántas estrellas hay en el cielo? (How many stars are in the sky?)

¡Cincuenta! (Fifty!)

Of course, we know that this answer isn't true! That's why the number 50 is a really silly answer. This joke uses the sound of words to create a pun. *Cincuenta* means 50, but *sin cuenta* means "countless."

12

# EXAGGERATED HUMOR

A **parody** is a silly imitation of someone or something. Parodies can take many shapes and forms. From a comedian doing a bad imitation of Arnold Schwarzenegger's Austrian accent, to a **reimagined** version of the famous painting *Mona Lisa* that features the pictured woman taking a selfie, parodies all have one thing in common. They are designed to give the audience a hilarious spin on the original.

# SIGHT GAG

A **sight gag** is a joke that doesn't rely on words at all. Sight gags use images or pictures to tell a joke. This type of joke gets a quick response from an audience, since the punch line is obvious right away. This is the perfect type of joke for artists and comic book authors.

# SONG PARODY

Parodies can also take the form of song. In the early 1950s, a folk song about a mountain called "On Top of Old Smokey" was topping the charts. Little more than a decade later, the song was re-written with hilarious lyrics. The original started with the line "On top of Old Smokey, all covered with snow…" The new version changed the lyrics to: "On top of spaghetti, all covered with cheese, I lost my poor meatball, when somebody sneezed…"

Q What English word is always pronounced wrong?

A Wrong!

Sorry son, but there's no eye in team.

## FUNNY BONE:

A gag reel, or blooper reel, is a collection of errors and mistakes made during a television show or movie. Even if the show isn't funny, the reel can be hilarious if it shows actors flubbing lines or bursting out in laughter. Some movies show blooper scenes at the end of the credits.

13

# LAUGHTER REALLY IS CONTAGIOUS

Famous English author Charles Dickens once said, "There is nothing in the world so irresistibly **contagious** as laughter." Have you ever noticed that as soon as your best friend starts to laugh, you feel like laughing, too? That's because laughter really is contagious. This means that when you hear someone laugh, even if you didn't hear the joke that made them chuckle, chances are that you'll be smiling soon enough! This happens because the sound of laughter triggers a response in your brain that causes your face to respond with a smile.

## IT'S GOOD FOR YOU

Unlike other things that are contagious, like a runny nose or a nasty cough, laughing is actually *good* for you, too! When you laugh out loud, you improve blood flow (which is important for your health) *and* you improve your body's ability to fight off disease! So go on, laugh your way to better health!

**Q** Where is the world's biggest rope?

**A** Europe.

**Q** What do you call a Roman with allergies?

**A** Julius Sneezer.

14

# LOL-ING AROUND THE WORLD

While the sound of laughter can be understood around the world, regardless of language barriers, what does laughter look like when it's written? Or texted, for that matter! While text message laughing in North America can range from "haha" to "hehe" to the traditional "LOL," other countries use different ways to communicate laughter through text. In France, "MDR" or "*mort de rire*" is the most popular way to laugh through text. It translates to "I'm dying of laughter!" In Thailand, texters simply write "55555." The number 5 is pronounced "ha" in Thai, so writing the number over and over suggests laughter! In Spanish, texters often write "*jajaja*," since the letter J is pronounced in Spanish like the English sound for the letter H.

Signs can be funny in any language:

ROAD CLOSED

 **Which English word becomes shorter when it is lengthened?**

Ⓐ Short.

**Attention Dog Guardians**

Pick up after your dogs - Thank you.

**Attention Dogs**

Grrrr, bark, woof. Good dog.

**FUNNY BONE:**

Sometimes, the best comedians have a signature joke, routine, or gag that gets the audience laughing every time. This is sometimes called their shtick. This expression comes from a Yiddish word meaning piece. When someone asks you "What's your shtick?" they're asking you to tell them your gimmick or trademark gag.

# CHAPTER 4
# METAPHORICALLY SPEAKING...

**Have you ever been told that you're a real barrel of laughs?**
This is an example of a metaphor, and it means that you're pretty funny! Metaphors are a great way to compare two things without using the words "like" or "as." Of course, you know that you're not actually a wooden barrel filled with the sound of laughter! Metaphors are a way to pay someone a compliment (or an insult), and also to describe places or things in interesting ways.

## METAPHORS AND MEANINGS

Metaphors are often used in humor when comparing two things. When the comparison is clever or unexpected, they make people chuckle. Metaphors are common to many languages and cultures. But depending on your location, metaphoric expressions can mean very different things. Take, for example, the expression "My teacher is a real cow!" In North America, this expression could make your classmates laugh, but it would not please your teacher. This wisecrack is considered an insult, and a mean-spirited one at that. However, in Japan, calling a teacher a cow has an entirely different meaning! It would be considered a compliment, as cows are considered to be hard-working and tireless creatures.

**Q** What do the Irish call a fake stone?

**A** A sham rock!

# INTERNATIONAL IDIOMS

While everyone can get a good laugh from a subject that doesn't hurt or offend, not all expressions translate between languages or cultures. Idioms are another form of figurative language. They're a type of metaphor that sound more like a saying or a true figure of speech. They are funny because they have a literal meaning, or their exact or basic meaning, but they also have a figurative, or symbolic, meaning. An idiom says one thing, but means another. Take weather-related idioms, for example. Have you ever heard someone say "It's raining cats and dogs?" To North Americans, this simply means that it's raining pretty hard outside. But around the world, many places have their own idioms for this kind of weather. Check them out:

In France they say "It's raining frogs."
(In French: *Il pleut des grenouilles.*)

In Portugal, they say "It's raining pocket knives."
(In Portuguese: *Está chovendo canivetes.*)

In the Netherlands, they say "It's raining old women."
(In Dutch: *Het regent oude wijven.*)

## FUNNY BONE:
To avoid offending people, or confusing your audience, try sticking to metaphors that have universal appeal when telling jokes. Compare the hot weather to a furnace. You can exclaim, "who turned the heat up in here?" when stepping outdoors, and nobody will be hurt or offended. Everyone can relate to the weather.

**Q** What do you call a fake noodle?

An Impasta. **A**

# AN IDIOM IN EVERY LANGUAGE?

Idioms aren't just about the weather. They can describe all kinds of situations. Some common English idioms are "Everyone is jumping on the bandwagon" or "I have a frog in my throat." Idioms in other languages and cultures are fun, too. Take these international idioms for example:

While we say "When pigs fly!" when we think something is *never* going to happen, the French say, "When chickens have teeth!" (*"Quand les poules auront des dents!"*)

In North America, the expression "I really put my foot in my mouth" means that you have said something you shouldn't have. In Finland, they say "I really let a frog out of my mouth!" (*"Päästää sammakko suusta."*)

When we're not kidding, we'll often say "I'm not pulling your leg." In Russia, the expression brings a funnier image to mind. Russians say "I'm not hanging noodles off your ears." (*"вешать лапшу на уши."*)

## FUNNY BONE:

There are many ways to deliver a joke, but one popular way to secure a laugh is to assume a deadpan expression. This means that when you tell a joke, your face and body should remain expressionless. Don't react to your own joke. Don't even laugh a little! The term originated in the 1920s. The word itself is made up of two parts. Dead in this case means expressionless, and pan is a slang term for face. The contrast between a funny one-liner and a straight face is always hilarious.

# LITERAL AND FIGURATIVE

If you take idioms literally, you may be missing the point. While idioms have a literal translation, they often cause a funny picture to appear in your mind. If you say it is raining cats and dogs, you don't expect anyone to believe cats and dogs are actually falling from the clouds. Determining the origin of these sayings is difficult, and sometimes impossible. They are often unique to a culture or country. As cultural sayings, they tend to be passed from **generation** to generation without anyone questioning their literal meaning. Anyone but a comic that is! Comics and comedians tend to question things for humor. Asking an audience to imagine the **mayhem** involved if it really (or literally) rained cats and dogs would generate a few laughs.

**Q** What does a nosy pepper do?

**A** Gets jalapeño business!

**Q** What happened to the dog that swallowed a firefly?

**A** It barked with de-light!

19

# CHAPTER 5
# CINNAMON AND ANTONIA

**Every language contains words that are related to one another.** There are many ways to describe these word-relationships. Synonyms, antonyms, and homonyms represent just a few of them. English **evolved** from many different languages, and we can sometimes see relationships between other languages and ours. So, do jokes using synonyms, antonyms, and homonyms translate between languages? Read on to find out!

## SYNONYMS AND HOMONYMS

Synonyms are words that have the same meaning. For example, travel and voyage can mean the same thing. Synonyms can be used cleverly in humor. In fact, they're often used as the basis for a good pun. Check this one out:

**My math teacher said that I was average. How mean!**

In this case, mean and average are synonyms, since they both describe the average number from a set of numbers in math! This joke also uses a homonym. Homonyms are words that sound the same, but have different meanings. The word "mean" is a math term that means to find the average, and an adjective describing something that isn't nice!

Homonyms work well when used in jokes that can play off of both meanings. Here's another example:

Why do we call pirates pirates?

Because they arrrrrr!

Two different uses of "arrrrrr" make this funny: the traditional sound a pirate makes, and a play on the word "are," meaning "to be."

# HOMOPHONE PHONE HOME

Homophones are words that sound like, or are pronounced like, other words, but have different meanings and spellings. One way to remember homophones is to use a few in a sentence. Of course, a homophone-loaded sentence requires concentration to write. As an added bonus, it might also be funny. Here are some examples:

**Charlie and her friends entered the maize maze. They had never been there before but they knew it was new and located beside the bean field.**

Can you find the homophones in those two sentences?

**Q** What do you get when you drop a blue hat into the Red Sea?

**A** A wet hat!

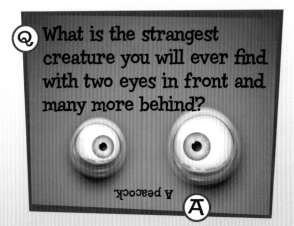

**Q** What is the strangest creature you will ever find with two eyes in front and many more behind?

**A** A peacock.

**FUNNY BONE:**
Stand-up comedy, a type of comedy routine in which a single comedian stands on a stage and tells jokes to the audience, has been around for a while. It can be traced to the early 1900s vaudeville theaters in New York City. Back then, standard comedy routines included the traditional pie-to-the-face gag. Today, stand-up comedy can be found at international festivals all over the world, from Edinburgh Festival Fringe in Scotland, to the Melbourne International Comedy Festival in Australia.

## NOTHING IN COMMON

Unlike synonyms and homonyms, antonyms are words that don't have anything in common. In fact, they are two words that are exact opposites. Antonyms are great for use in jokes when you're telling a riddle. Remember, riddles are poems or sayings that confuse the audience, because they have many possible answers...but only one answer that is clever and true!

## LOST IN TRANSLATION

Each language has a unique origin, and its own word-relationships. Jokes using synonyms, antonyms, and homonyms aren't only used in the English language. But synonyms, antonyms, and homonyms don't always translate well into other languages, because once the words are translated, they often lose their double meanings.

**Q** What has 50 heads and 50 tails?

**A** 50 pennies!

**Q** What falls but never breaks, and breaks but never falls?

**A** Night and day!

22

**Q** What does a frog eat in Paris?

**A** French flies!

**Q** What is Medusa's favorite cheese?

**A** Gorgon-zola!

# FUNNY BONE:

Did you know that some people actually study humor in university? They do research on humor and its role in entertainment, business, and health. They also study why people find certain things funny, and whether it depends on their culture or age. Humor scholars even have organizations such as the International Society for Humor Studies. They also have annual conferences and journals on humor research. Funny that!

# CHAPTER 6
# AROUND THE WORLD FUN AND GAMES

**While jokes based on wordplay can get lost in translation, some jokes really are universal.** Jokes that don't rely on language at all can be particularly appealing to people all over the world. Sometimes, humor is rooted in the traditions of a country and can teach you a lot about the world around you.

## FUNNY BONE:

Ever notice how some kids are terrified of painted circus or parade clowns? Some adults dread clowns as well. This fear of clowns is called coulrophobia. People who fear clowns can feel panicky around them. This is sometimes because clown costumes and makeup are often dramatic. They are designed to exaggerate facial features, which can remind some people of monsters.

## CLOWNING AROUND

From ancient Egypt to Imperial China, it seems like nearly everyone has something (or someone!) funny in common: the clown. Clowns were created to entertain and poke fun at ordinary life situations. A lot of what clowns do is physical or visual humor, and it doesn't rely on language. Whether it was a court jester entertaining kings and queens centuries ago, or a mime with a painted white face working at street festivals today, clowns sure have a way of getting around.

**Q** Where do clowns go to college?

Har-Har-Harvard

**A**

# LET'S GO TO CLOWN SCHOOL!

So you want to be a clown? Clowns are performers who excel in the comic arts of slapstick and physical humor. They make everyday things seem ridiculous by their exaggerated antics. Here are some clown school tips on playing the fool:

1.  **Don't try to be funny:** This sounds like bad advice, but it really means "be yourself." Clowns are performers. They see the world around them and poke fun at things. You want to develop a clown personality that feels comfortable.

2.  **Practice your funny face:** Now, this doesn't mean just your funny face. Use a mirror and learn how to exaggerate a sad face, scared face, or confused face. Once you've got a number of faces mastered, try using them in comic situations, such as when your parent or guardian asks you to clean your room (cue **outrageous** scared face).

3.  **Go ahead, be awkward:** Clowns know that being human, with human **frailties**, such as being clumsy or feeling out of place, can be used for humor. Learn how to trip dramatically, or stand alone with an **elaborate** strangeness.

4.  **Clown clothes:** You don't need a red nose, white face, enormous shoes, or bowtie to be a clown. If you've mastered your clown faces and exaggerated posing, you can make any bit of clothing into a clown costume. Just make it fit your clown personality. Try a crazy hat or a ridiculous moustache.

5.  **Clown skills:** All clowns have special talents or skills that they work on. Yours could be telling jokes, juggling socks, walking weirdly, or singing silly songs about your family members! Whatever you do, practice your clown skills until you know them by heart.

**Q** What's the pink stuff between a circus elephant's toes?

**A** Slow clowns.

25

## ANCIENT COMEDY

Some nations have a long history of laughter. In Greece, comedy dates back to the 6th century B.C., when a festival was held to honor the Greek god Dionysus. At this festival, three types of performances emerged: tragedy, comedy, and the **satyr** play. In Ancient Greek comedies, there were no more than four actors, and they had to wear masks and elaborate costumes so that they could play multiple roles. They performed in open-air theaters for thousands of audience members!

## MASKING HUMOR

In the late 1500s, a form of comedic performance developed in Italy. *Comedia dell'arte*, which translates to "comedy of the professional artists," was performed outdoors. Each actor had a specific role to play. They wore traditional masks, and no matter what play they were performing, the same characters always emerged. These characters, often called "stock" characters, included *Il Capitano* (the captain, or soldier), *Il Dottore* (the doctor), and *La Ruffiana* (an old woman or town gossip).

*Comedia dell'arte mask*

### FUNNY BONE:

We still see stock characters in movies, television, and theater today. A stock character is familiar and immediately recognizable. Today's stock characters include the geek, the jock, and the popular girl. Stock characters can be useful in comedies because they are exaggerated versions of reality, but we need to be careful when using stock characters, because (don't forget!) they really are just stereotypes.

Q

**What do smart Canadians get on tests?**

A  All eh's.

# THAT'S A FUNNY NAME!

Sometimes, it isn't the comedic styles or history of a location that make you laugh. Occasionally, it's the name of the location itself! Check out this list for a gut-busting collection of place names that will remind you the world is a very funny place!

| Place Name | Fun Fact |
| --- | --- |
| Llanfairpwllgwyngyllgogerychwyrn-drobwllllantysiliogogogoch, Wales | Called Llanfairpwll for short, this village is located on the island of Anglesey, in Wales. |
| Middlefart, Denmark | This town's name is composed of the old Danish word *mæthal* meaning "middle" and *far* meaning "way." |
| Santa Claus, Indiana | This town was originally called Santa Fe, but once they found out there was already a town by that name, they had to re-name themselves, and quick! |
| Eighty Eight, Kentucky | The town was named in the 1860s by Dabney Nunnally, who came up with the name by emptying his pocket and counting 88 cents. |
| Eyebrow, Saskatchewan | This town is named for the eyebrow-shaped hill nearby! |
| Little Snoring, Norfolk, England | Little Snoring is actually *bigger* than Great Snoring, which is a smaller village located two miles to the south! |

# CHAPTER 7
# YOUR GUIDE TO FUNNY

**Whether you live in Sandwich, Illinois, St. Louis-du-Ha! Ha!, Quebec, or Middlefart, Denmark, you can be the funniest kid on the block!** Being funny has nothing to do with how many people you know, or how many places you've been. It's about seeing the lighter side of things, and looking for a laugh in all that you do.

## FUNNY BONE:

Comic strips made their appearance in American newspapers in the late 1800s. In 1897, Rudolf Dirks, a German immigrant, published his comic strip called The Katzenjammer Kids. He is credited with being the first comic strip artist to use speech bubbles.

Q Why is it so hard to borrow money from a leprechaun?

A They are always a little short.

Q What has four eyes but cannot see?

A Mississippi.

# WHAT MAKES FOR FUNNY?

So, what is universally funny? Is there a joke, gag, or routine that will make everyone laugh? Probably not (you win some, you lose some), but that doesn't mean that comedy can't be figured out. What an audience will find funny is usually familiar, or unfamiliar, and expected (or unexpected). Comedy is full of **contradictions**, but always contains an element of truth. Confused? Try following these simple tips, so that you can be sure to get a laugh every time.

1. **Don't give the joke away (a.k.a. the element of surprise).** Comedy is all about leading the audience one way, and then suddenly leading them in another. While the punch line is the best part of a joke, if you give it away too soon, your audience won't get a kick out of the surprise. Give them time to think about it.

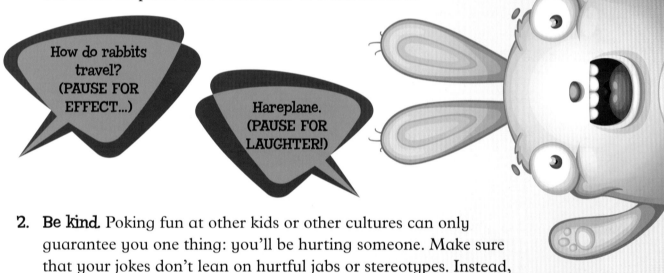

How do rabbits travel? (PAUSE FOR EFFECT...)

Hareplane. (PAUSE FOR LAUGHTER!)

2. **Be kind.** Poking fun at other kids or other cultures can only guarantee you one thing: you'll be hurting someone. Make sure that your jokes don't lean on hurtful jabs or stereotypes. Instead, focus on topics that give everyone something to laugh about!

3. **It's all in the delivery!** The best formula for delivering a joke includes a clear voice and some sort of facial or body expression. Find a way to make an impact.

4. **Remember your lines.** Since delivery is crucial, memorizing your jokes will be your best bet at getting laughs. Try practicing your jokes in front of the mirror, or better yet, for your family pet!

5. **Be your silly self!** Don't forget that your jokes should reflect who you are as a comedian. Tell jokes about the topics that interest you, and don't take yourself too seriously. If nobody laughs, it's okay! Simply pause, give a little chuckle, and move on.

# CHAPTER 8
# FIND OUT MORE

**Loving the humor game?** Can't get enough? For more joke ideas, tips, and information on all things funny, check out these sources.

## BOOKS:

Elliott, Rob. *Laugh-Out-Loud Jokes for Kids*. Revell, 2010.

Leno, Jay. *How to Be the Funniest Kid in the Whole Wide World*. Simon & Schuster, 2005.

Perl, Erica S. *Chicken Butt*. Abrams Books for Young Readers, 2009.

## WEBSITES:

www.kidsjokesoftheday.com
This website is full of one-liners, puns, riddles, knock-knock jokes, and everything in between!

www.jokesbykids.com
Let's see how well you've been paying attention. This website lets you submit your very own jokes! Reveal your funny talents to the world, and get a kick out of what others have shared, too.

# HALL OF HUMOR

## Astérix

Astérix is a popular French comic book character that made its debut in 1959. The stories, written and illustrated by a French duo, are deeply rooted in the history of European culture. Astérix comes from Gaul, a region from over 2,000 years ago that included present-day France. Astérix has many silly and crazy adventures along the way, including winning a gold medal in the Olympics! Astérix's adventures have appeared in many books and films, both animated and live action.

## Charlie Chaplin

Famous for his comic portrayal of a "**tramp**," Charlie Chaplin is considered one of the greatest comedians of all time. He was born in London, England in 1889, and began his career at the age of ten as a talented tap dancer. Chaplin rose to stardom during the silent film era, when actors had to rely on sight gags and slapstick humor instead of words for laughs. He appeared in over 80 films, won an Honorary Academy Award in 1972, and lived until 1977.

*Astérix is so popular in France that the cartoon even appears as street art.*

32 USA

Charlie Chaplin's Little Tramp

1998

*Chaplin's tramp character has been honored on stamps, art murals, statues, and as a wax figure.*

# GLOSSARY

**Note:** Some boldfaced terms are defined where they appear in the text

**contagious** Something spread from one person to another

**culture** The customs, art, and ideas of a specific country, people, or social group

**deadpan** Humor that is amusing while attempting to be serious

**contradictions** Ideas that are opposed to each other, or the opposite

**elaborate** Detailed and complicated in design or planning

**evolved** Something that has developed or changed gradually

**frailties** Things that are weak and delicate

**figurative language** Language that is not literal, or that means something different than the actual definition

**generation** A group of people born or living at about the same time

**gorgon** In Greek mythology, three sisters who had snakes for hair, and the ability to turn anyone who looked at them into stone

**heyday** A time of highest strength or success

**insulting** Disrespectful and offensive

**mayhem** Something that is disordered and often confusing

**outrageous** Shocking, bold, or wildly improbable

**reimagined** Rethinking something to remake it into something else

**satyr** A type of comic play from ancient Greece that included many gags and pranks

**stereotypes** Widely held views of people or things that are often incorrect, oversimplified, or disrespectful

**tramp** A person who travels from place to place looking for work, and who often looks scruffy or messy

**universal** Something common to all people and many cultures

**wordplay** Witty use of the multiple meanings of words, especially the use of puns

# INDEX